Is there a dinosaur under my school?

Is there a dinosaur under my school?

ISABEL THOMAS

Collins

Contents

Chapter 1 Buried treasure 6

Bonus: Megalodon 22

Chapter 2 What kind of rock? 24

Bonus: Rock key 38

Chapter 3 Is it old enough? 40

Bonus: Rock and fossil jokes 56

Chapter 4 Did dinosaurs ever live here? 58

Chapter 5 Finding fossils without digging . . 72

Bonus: Interview with Mary Anning 84

Chapter 6 Finding fossils INSIDE your school! . . . 86

Bonus: Surprising sedimentary rocks 102

Glossary 104

About the author 106

Book chat 108

CHAPTER 1
Buried treasure

In 2022, pupils at a school in Los Angeles, US, got a gigantic surprise.

Builders had been working at San Pedro High School for almost a year. Pupils were looking forward to getting three new buildings full of high-tech classrooms. In June 2022, diggers rolled into the central courtyard, where the children usually ate lunch.

No one expected what happened next.

As the excavators began digging, they hit a layer of solid rock. Embedded in the rock were thousands of fossil shells.

The builders reported what they had found. The very next morning, an excited **palaeontologist** arrived at the site.

Over the next two years, millions more fossils were carefully collected from the rocks beneath the school. They included the fossils of sabre-toothed fish, sea turtles and giant sharks known as megalodons, which had lived in that part of the world millions of years ago.

It makes you wonder ... might there be fossils hidden beneath YOUR school, too? Could they include megalodon teeth, or even dinosaur bones?

Luckily, you don't have to start digging to find out. Palaeontologists use clues to predict where dinosaur fossils are most likely to be found. These clues can help you to predict the chances of there being a dinosaur under your school.

- What kind of rock is my school built on?
- How old is the rock?
- Where in the world is my school ... and did dinosaurs live here in the past?

Chapters 2, 3 and 4 will help you answer these questions. But first, you'll need to know exactly what fossils are, and how they form. Your dinosaur hunt starts here ...

Digging into words

It's not just rocks. Words often contain clues about their origins, too! For example, the word 'fossil' comes from the Latin word *fossilis* meaning 'dug up'. Look out for these boxes for more examples.

Palaeontologists uncover fossils at San Pedro High School.

What are fossils?

Fossils are special rocks that formed thousands, millions or even billions of years ago. They are special because they show us the shape of plants and animals that lived (and died) at that time.

Living things come in all shapes and sizes, so fossils are found in all shapes and sizes too.

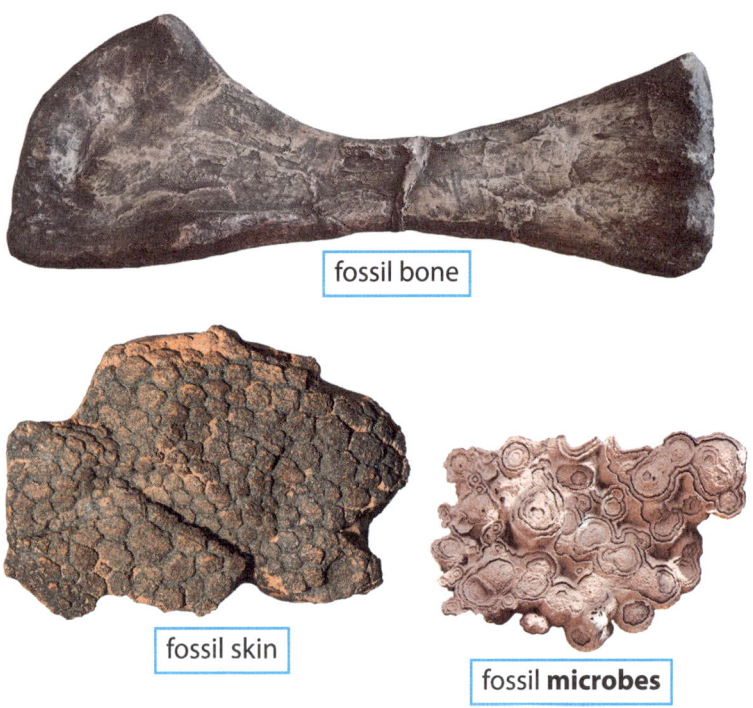

fossil bone

fossil skin

fossil **microbes**

What can fossils show us?

Fossils show how life on our planet has changed over time.

Today, Earth's largest animals are mammals. They include enormous elephants on land, and whales in the ocean.

Fossils show that millions of years ago, the biggest animals on Earth were not elephants and whales, but gigantic reptile-like creatures. They included lumbering dinosaurs on land, and ichthyosaurs (known as 'fish-lizards') in the oceans. Today, these creatures are **extinct**.

an ichthyosaur fossil

Fossils also show us how Earth itself has changed. Plant fossils tell us that parts of the world that are now scorching deserts or frigid ice caps were once hot, wet and covered in jungle. Fossils have even helped scientists prove that Earth's rocks and land move around over time!

However, reading the clues found in fossils is not easy.

artist's impression of an ichthyosaur

Jumbled jigsaws

Fossils are usually found inside rocks. Sometimes, almost all the bones of an ancient animal are found. Scientists can put them back together like a giant jigsaw.

But most fossils don't look like they do in museums. They are often jumbled together with fossils from lots of other creatures. There might be just one or two bones from a particular creature, and those bones might be broken up into fragments.

To understand more about **prehistoric** animals, scientists compare fossils to animals that are alive today. This helps them work out what the extinct animals might have looked like. It also helps them to estimate each animal's size and weight, and how old it was when it died.

But what if the animal doesn't look like any of today's animals?

A mysterious monster

Hundreds of years ago, strange fossil bones were found in a quarry near Oxford, UK. They included a giant leg bone, a few **vertebrae** and a piece of jaw with a few teeth. They didn't match the skeleton of any living animal. Were they from a mammoth? Or some kind of ancient hippo?

In the early 1800s, an expert called William Buckland began to look at the fossils. With the help of a famous illustrator, Mary Morland, he tried to work out what kind of creature the bones belonged to.

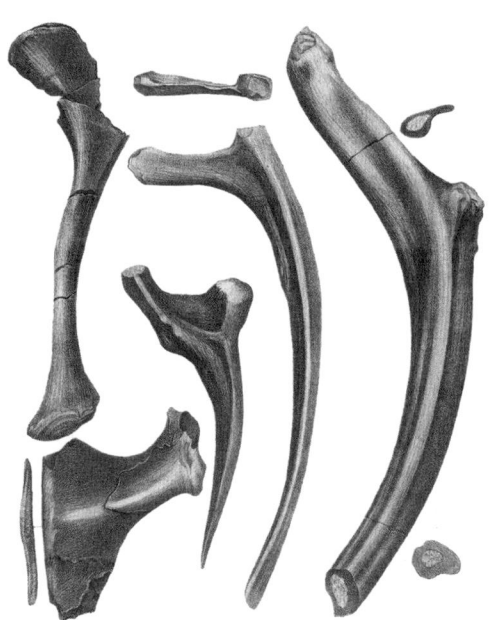

The teeth reminded them of lizards – but much bigger. They assumed that the animal walked on four legs, in the same way lizards do. They imagined a 12-metre long reptile, with the head of a crocodile and a sturdy body like a rhinoceros. It was named Megalosaurus.

Digging into words

In Ancient Greek, *megas* means big or great, and *sauros* means lizard. 'Megalosaurus' combines the two ideas to create a word meaning 'great lizard'.

Over the next 20 years, people found more fossils with similar features. One of the creatures was named Iguanodon. In 1841, palaeontologist Richard Owen realised these animals were very different from lizards. He said that they probably walked on two legs, not four. He suggested that Megalosaurus and Iguanodon belonged in a brand new group of animals – the dinosaurs.

Digging into words

Owen invented the word 'dinosauria', to call these animals 'fearfully great' lizards. However, the Ancient Greek word *deinos* means 'terrible', so dinosaur actually means 'terrible lizard'.

At first, people thought Megalosaurus looked like this.

New clues

Since the 1800s, more fossils of Megalosaurus and hundreds of other dinosaurs have been found. Some have been found in quarries and professional digs, but others have been discovered by accident, in school playgrounds and back gardens!

They include bones and teeth, as well as fossil footprints and even fossil poos, known as coprolites! Fossil footprints can reveal how dinosaurs walked, and small fossils found inside coprolites can reveal what they ate.

In 2025, researchers found 200 fossil dinosaur footprints at a quarry in Oxfordshire. They include three-toed footprints made by Megalosaurus!

Now, Palaeontologists use new technology to help them study fossils. Researchers recently used a scanner to examine the Megalosaurus fossils that Mary Morland drew. They spotted five teeth that no one had noticed before. Palaeontologists have even found clues that Megalosaurus might have been covered in fluffy feathers!

Today people think Megalosaurus looked like this.

What can't fossils show us?

Even today, no one can be sure that we are drawing dinosaurs correctly. Usually, fossils only show us what the hard parts of an animal's body looked like. Bones and teeth can't tell us the colour of a dinosaur's skin or feathers, or what noises a dinosaur made. Palaeontologists must guess, based on the animals that we know today.

Dinosaur mania

The more scientists have discovered about dinosaurs, the more popular they've become! Dinosaurs star in movies, TV programmes and video games and decorate clothes and lunchboxes. Many people dream of discovering a dinosaur fossil.

So, could a dinosaur fossil be hidden under your school?

To find out, we need to discover how fossils get inside rocks in the first place …

The *Jurassic World* movies imagine what would happen if dinosaurs were alive today!

Bonus

Megalodon

Megalodon was the largest shark that ever lived. The oldest megalodon fossils are around 23 million years old. The youngest megalodon fossils are 2.6 million years old, which tells us this shark became extinct fairly recently, compared to the dinosaurs.

Megalodon grew up to 24.3 metres long.

Digging into words
The name 'megalodon' combines the Ancient Greek words *megalos* (large or great) and *odon* (tooth), to mean 'large tooth'.

A bite ten times stronger than a great white's.

No one has ever found a complete megalodon skeleton, but fossils of its teeth can tell us lots about this enormous shark.

great white shark

Jaws that could open wide enough to swallow a car!

276 serrated teeth that grew up to 18 centimetres long.

Megalodon replaced its teeth every couple of weeks, getting through 40,000 teeth in a lifetime.

Fossil bones of giant whales have been found with megalodon toothmarks on!

CHAPTER 2
What kind of rock?

So, you want to know if a fossilised dinosaur is hiding out under your school?

First, you need to know what kind of rock your school is built on – because fossils are only found in certain types of rock. To understand why, let's look at how rocks form, and how they come to have fossils hidden inside them.

Rock families

There are thousands of different kinds of rocks. Scientists group them into three main 'families'. Each is formed in a different way. But can you spot what all three have in common?

Family: Igneous rocks

Examples: granite, obsidian, pumice

Formed from: **molten** rock (such as lava)

How? Molten rock cools and becomes solid, like melted chocolate setting.

granite

Family: Sedimentary rocks

Examples: sandstone, chalk, limestone

Formed from: tiny pieces of other rocks (sediments)

How? Sediments sink to the bottom of a lake or ocean in layers; over time, they get squashed together and become rock.

chalk

Family: Metamorphic rocks

Examples: marble, slate

Formed from: any type of rock

How? Rock gets heated up without melting completely, and changes into a different type of rock.

marble

So, what do all rocks have in common?

Every rock is formed from other types of rock! This is why it's rare to find a rock that is as old as Earth itself (more than four billion years old). Rocks are constantly being broken down by wind and water, or changed by heat and pressure, forming new types of rock. This process is called the rock cycle.

The rock cycle

The rock cycle describes how old rocks get transformed into new rocks. Any type of rock can be changed into any other type of rock.

Sometimes the rock cycle involves rapid changes. When molten lava cools down quickly (becoming solid in just a few minutes) it can form a black, glassy igneous rock called obsidian.

Usually, the change from one type of rock to another happens very slowly. It takes hundreds, thousands or even millions of years for sediments to become sedimentary rock.

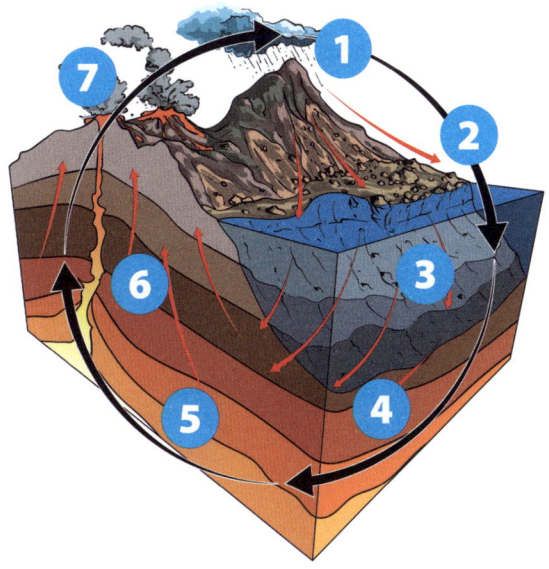

1. Rocks of all kinds are worn away by wind and rain, forming mud, clay and sand (sediments).

2. Sediments get washed into rivers, lakes and oceans. They sink to the bottom and build up in layers.

3. Over time, the deepest sediments become squeezed together. They become sedimentary rock.

4. Deep underground, rocks are heated by Earth's core. Heating and squeezing can change igneous or sedimentary rocks into metamorphic rocks.

5. Some rocks are heated and squeezed so much, they melt completely to form magma.

6. Some magma cools slowly underground to form igneous rock.

7. Some magma pushes up and flows out of volcanoes as lava. The lava cools quickly to form igneous rock.

Where is each type of rock found?

All three kinds of rock can be found almost anywhere in the world. Your school might be built on igneous, sedimentary or metamorphic rock.

This doesn't matter … unless you are looking for fossils!

Fossils are only found in sedimentary rocks. To find out why, let's zoom back in time and watch a dinosaur fossil form.

Digging into words

The three rock families are named using Latin and Greek words that describe how they form. The word *sedimentum* means 'sinking down'. Igneous means 'made of fire', and metamorphic means 'changing form'.

From bone to stone

100 million years ago …

… a dinosaur dies.

It sinks to the bottom of a shallow lake.

Over time, the soft parts of the dinosaur decay and disappear. Layers of mud, sand and other sediments settle on top, protecting the hard parts such as the bones and teeth.

Millions of years later …

The sediments are squeezed together by the pressure of all the layers above. They harden into rock around the bones.

As water trickles through the sediments, **minerals** from the bones seep out into the rock. They are replaced with different minerals. New rock forms in the shape of the bones.

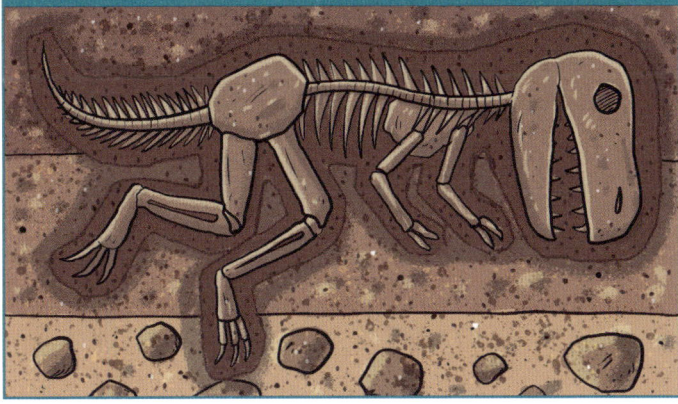

Not every prehistoric creature was fossilised. In fact, it was quite rare. Fossils can only form when a living thing is quickly covered in sediments after it dies. Those sediments become rock, creating a lasting record of the shape of the creature's bones.

What happens next?

The rock cycle shows us that sedimentary rock can either:

- stay as sedimentary rock
- get worn down by wind and water to become sediments again
- be heated and squeezed enough to change into metamorphic rock
- or become heated so much that it melts and then sets, to become igneous rock.

If sedimentary rock gets changed by the rock cycle, any fossils inside get destroyed. This is why fossils are not found in igneous or metamorphic rock.

If your school is built on sedimentary rock, there is a chance that the rock contains fossils! But how can you tell what kind of rock your school is built on?

What kind of rock?

Scientists who study rocks are called petrologists. They use clues to tell if a rock is sedimentary.

> **Digging into words**
> The name 'petrologist' comes from the Greek words *petros*, meaning 'rock', and *logos*, meaning 'study'.

Clue 1: Sedimentary rocks form in layers

Sedimentary rocks are formed from sediments that settled in layers at the bottom of a lake or sea. In some places, we can see these layers in the rock, so we know straight away they are sedimentary rocks.

Clue 2: Sedimentary rocks are made up of grains

In most places, the rocks of Earth's crust are covered by a deep layer of soil, but this soil often contains smaller chunks of the rocks beneath. If you inspect one of these smaller chunks, you might be able to see grains or crystals. Sedimentary rocks have rounded grains. The grains might be as large as pebbles, or too small to see with your eyes.

Sandstone formed from grains of sand that settled at the bottom of a shallow sea. Under a microscope, you can still see the grains of sand. Other minerals have filled the gaps between the grains, sticking them together like cement.

Clue 3: Some sedimentary rocks are soft and crumbly

Igneous and metamorphic rocks are made up of crystals. They are often very hard and difficult to break. Sedimentary rocks are softer and easier to break.

Shale and mudstone formed from very tiny grains of clay and mud. They are soft and crumbly.

Clue 4: Sedimentary rocks often contain fossils

Spotting fossils is a big clue that you are looking at sedimentary rock. This is because fossils form in sedimentary rock.

Limestone often contains fossils. In fact, some pieces of limestone are almost completely made up of fossils!

Case study

In 2025, with the help of his parents, seven-year-old Elliot cracked open limestone rocks in his garden in Matlock, England. He was amazed to find they were full of fossils of **Jurassic** sea creatures that lived 140 million years ago!

These fossils are similar to the ones Elliot found.

The type of fossils found in sedimentary rock depends on both the type of rock, and how old it is. In the next chapter, you'll find out how old the rock under your school must be to have a chance of discovering dinosaur fossils.

Rock key

Use this rock key to help identify rocks you find.

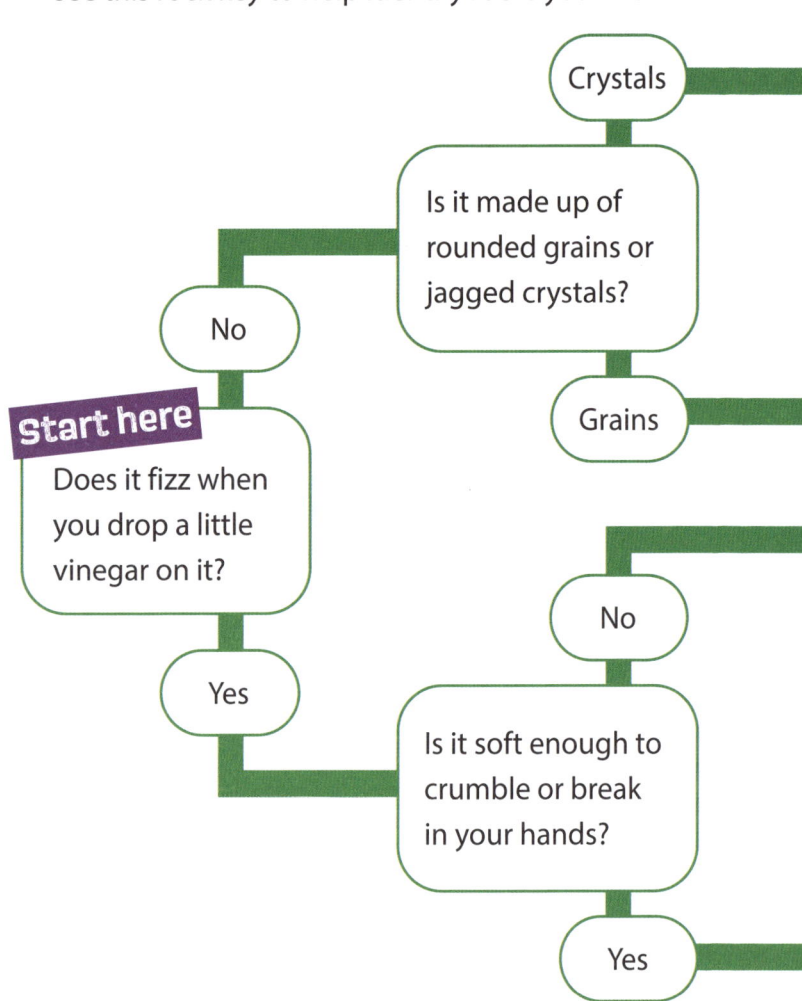

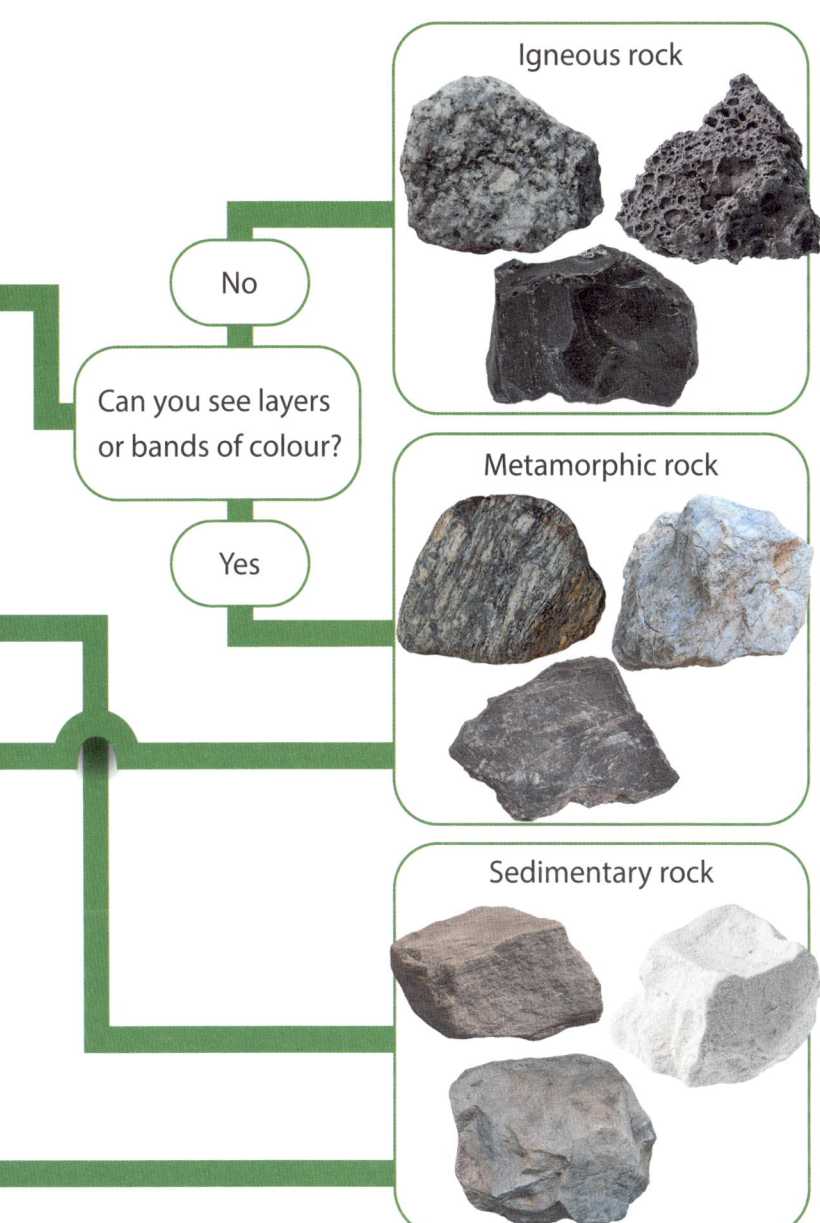

CHAPTER 3
Is it old enough?

If you've discovered your school is built on sedimentary rock, then there is a chance that the rock beneath your school contains fossils.

But could it contain *dinosaur* fossils?

To find out, you first need to know how old the rock is. Sedimentary rocks can only contain fossils of plants and animals that were alive at the same time the rock began to form.

Earth's oldest sedimentary rocks are almost FOUR BILLION years old. This is a mind-boggling number. Dinosaurs did not exist way back then, so those rocks don't contain any dinosaur fossils.

How big is a billion?
If you said one number every second, counting to one billion would take you almost 32 years.

Earth's youngest sedimentary rocks were formed just a few thousand years ago. Dinosaurs died out long before then, so those rocks don't contain any dinosaur fossils.

To find dinosaur fossils, we need to find sedimentary rocks that formed when the dinosaurs were alive.

The first dinosaurs lived around 230 million years ago.

The last dinosaurs died out about 66 million years ago.

Only sedimentary rocks formed during the 180 million years dinosaurs were alive can possibly contain dinosaur fossils.

But how on Earth can you tell the age of a rock?

How many birthdays have you had?

Layer upon layer

The first clue comes from the way that sedimentary rocks form in layers. Imagine sprinkling layers of sand into a bottle.

The top layers go in last. These layers are the youngest.

The bottom layers go in first. These layers are the oldest.

When scientists look at the layers in sedimentary rocks, they use the same rule. The lowest layers are the oldest. This means fossils found in deeper layers must be older than fossils found higher up.

In Argentina, an ancient river carved a deep valley through the sedimentary rock. This makes it possible to see the colourful layers of rock that are usually hidden beneath the surface. Each layer was formed at a different time.

Fossils found in deeper layers of rock are usually older. However, there is one problem with the layer rule. Rocks don't stick around forever in the place where they formed!

From bottom to top

Remember the rock cycle? Rocks on the surface are constantly being worn away by wind and weather. The top layers get worn away first. One by one, deeper layers find themselves on the surface. Fossils also appear on the surface in this way. This means scientists can't rely on layers alone. They need other ways to determine the age of rocks and fossils.

Natural clocks

All rocks are made up of different ingredients, called minerals. Some of these minerals change over time in a very steady way. By finding out how much they have changed, scientists can work out exactly how much time has passed since the rock formed.

Some rocks contain tiny crystals of a tough mineral called zircon. By looking at how much the zircon has changed, scientists can work out how old the rock is.

Earth's changing magnetic field also provides clues. The position of the magnetic North and South Pole switch every 300,000 years or so. This leaves behind traces in rocks.

Index fossils

Another clue to the age of rock comes from fossils themselves. Over time, scientists have learned that certain types of ammonites only lived on Earth for a short time. When they spot these 'index fossils' in a rock, it tells them how old the rock must be.

ammonite fossil

model of extinct ammonite

Ammonite fossils are found almost everywhere that oceans once existed. Scientists have named more than 10,000 different types! When scientists find ammonite fossils in rocks, it tells them the rock formed during the Jurassic or **Cretaceous** period. The type of ammonite can tell them exactly how old the rock is.

Dating dinosaurs

Not every creature that lived in the past formed a fossil. In fact, it was quite rare. But using clues from the fossils that have been found so far, scientists have mapped out the history of life on Earth – including the history of the dinosaurs.

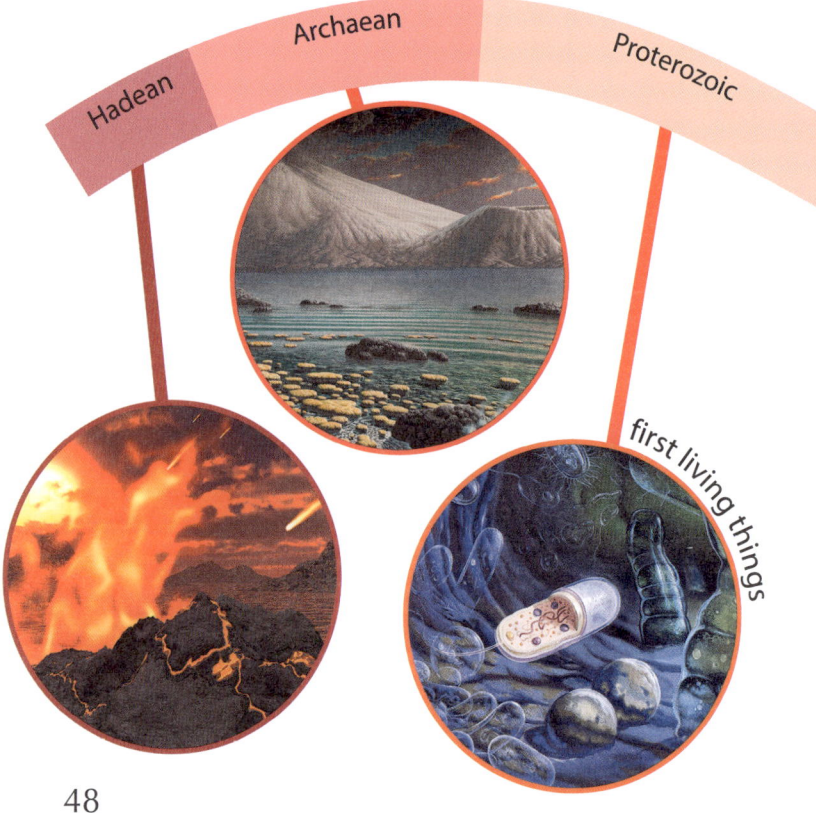

Hadean

Archaean

Proterozoic

first living things

If we find a sedimentary rock between 230 and 66 million years old, we know it might contain dinosaur fossils. If we know the exact age of the rock, we can even predict what TYPE of dinosaur fossils it might contain.

The period when dinosaurs ruled Earth is known as the Mesozoic. It lasted around 180 million years, but scientists divide it up into three shorter periods: The Triassic, the Jurassic and the Cretaceous. Different types of dinosaurs lived in each period.

The Triassic

Triassic rocks began forming more than 225 million years ago. They are the oldest rocks to contain dinosaur fossils, including Eoraptor and Herrerasaurus.

Herrerasaurus

The Triassic ended with a mysterious extinction event, when half of the animals on Earth died out. Most large reptiles became extinct, but dinosaurs survived. Now they had less competition for food and shelter. They grew in numbers and spread to live in new places.

Digging into words
The 'Triassic' was named after three layers of rocks formed at that time, which were found in Germany. The Greek word *trias* means 'group of three'.

Eoraptor

The Jurassic

The Jurassic period began about 200 million years ago and lasted about 55 million years. During this time, the world's weather became warmer and wetter. Fossils show us that hundreds of new types of dinosaurs appeared in the Jurassic period, including Allosaurus, Stegosaurus and Diplodocus.

Digging into words
'Jurassic' was named after the Jura mountains in France, which are made up mainly of limestone rock from that period.

The Cretaceous

The Cretaceous period lasted for 79 million years. That is nearly 400 times as long as humans have lived on Earth! During this long stretch of time, Earth's seas and oceans teemed with giant sharks and **marine** reptiles such as ichthyosaurs, mosasaurs and plesiosaurs. On land, Tyrannosaurus, Velociraptor and Triceratops ruled. The Cretaceous period ended with an asteroid strike that wiped out most dinosaurs.

Digging into words
'Cretaceous' was named after the Latin word *creta* meaning 'chalk-like'. Most of the world's chalk rock was formed in that period.

Mapping rocks

Colourful geological maps show which types of rock are found in a country or continent. The first geological map of a country was a map of Britain, drawn by William Smith more than 200 years ago. He used fossils to identify rocks from different periods.

If your school is built on Triassic, Jurassic or Cretaceous sedimentary rock, it might just be standing on dinosaur fossils too! There is just one question left to answer: did dinosaurs actually live in the part of the world where your school stands today?

1. Triassic rocks (shown in orange on the map). Triassic dinosaurs found in the UK include Asylosaurus and Thecodontosaurus.

2. The Jurassic Coast in Dorset, England, is famous for its Jurassic rocks and fossils (shown in yellow). Jurassic dinosaurs include Megalosaurus and Gigantosaurus.

3. Cretaceous rocks (shown in green). Cretaceous dinosaurs found in the UK include Baryonyx and Iguanodon.

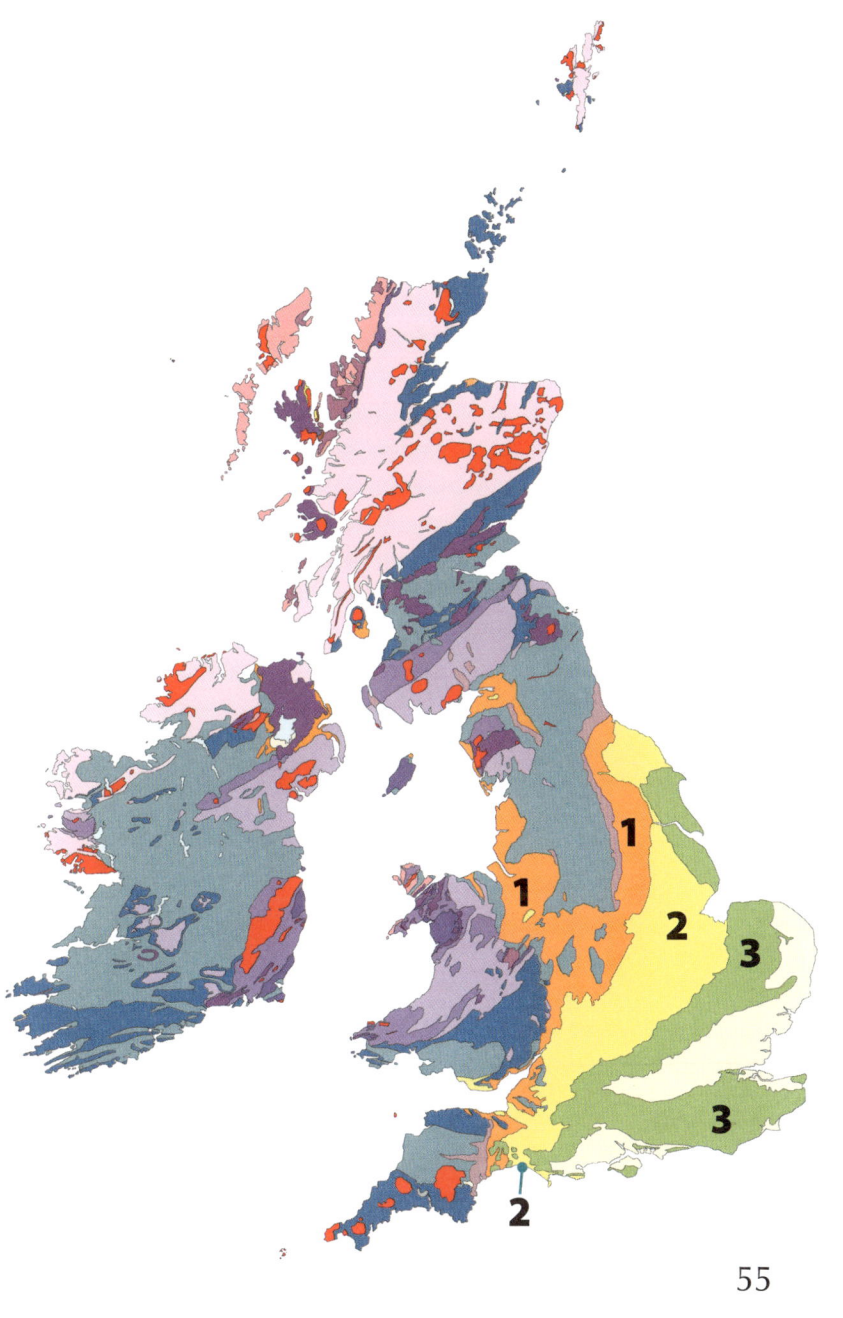

Bonus

Rock and fossil jokes

Why did the dinosaur cross the road?

The chicken hadn't evolved yet!

What makes more noise than a dinosaur?

Two dinosaurs!

CHAPTER 4
Did dinosaurs ever live here?

If your school is built on sedimentary rock that formed when dinosaurs were alive, there is a chance there might be dinosaur fossils under it.

The final thing you need to know is whether dinosaurs ever lived in the part of the world where your school stands now.

A changing planet

The fossils found under San Pedro High School in Los Angeles, US, were all fossils of ancient sea and seashore creatures.

This tells scientists that a shallow sea once covered the land where the school stands today. Today, Los Angeles is a giant city.

prehistoric dolphin

sabre-toothed salmon

megalodon

Earth's rocky surface feels stable under our feet but, in fact, our planet is always changing. Oceans rise and fall, ice sheets freeze and melt. Scientists have even found evidence that the continents themselves were once in totally different places!

Let's take a closer look …

Shifting landscapes

For a long time, people assumed that Earth's surface has always looked like it does today.

Scientists studying rocks and fossils were some of the first people to notice clues that this is not the case.

It also seemed strange that the eastern coasts of North and South America matched up with the western coasts of Europe and Africa – like two pieces of a giant jigsaw. Could it just be a coincidence?

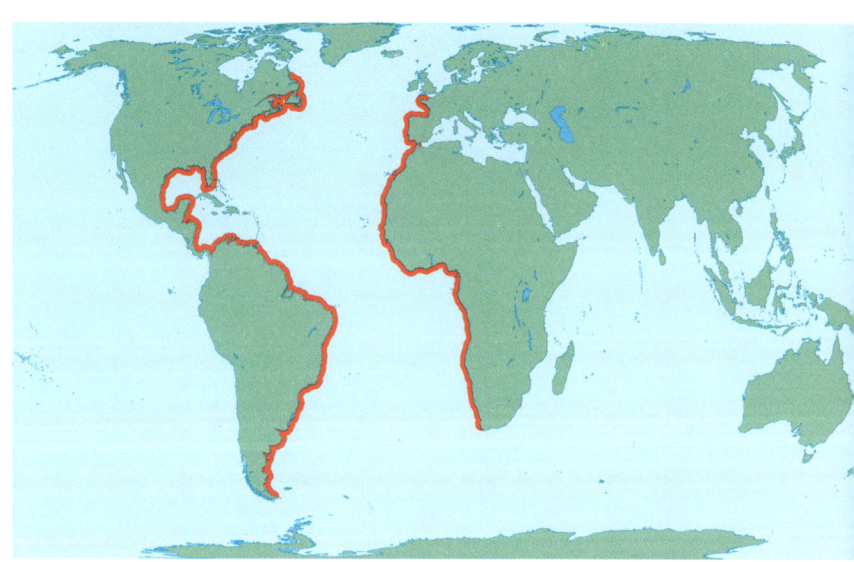

In the early 1900s, an **earth scientist** called Alfred Wegener realised these two different areas of the world – thousands of kilometres apart – had once been right next to each other.

Long before humans lived on Earth, all the land was part of one huge continent.

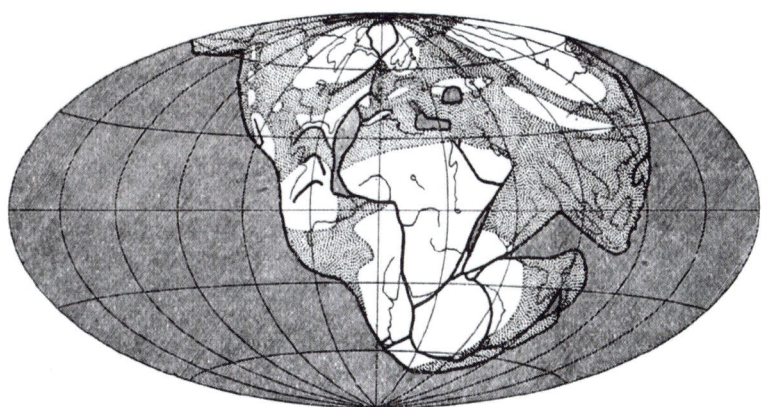

Alfred Wegener's map of Pangaea

Digging into words

Alfred called this supercontinent Pangaea, meaning 'all lands'. It is based on the Ancient Greek words *pan* (meaning 'all') and *gaia* (meaning 'Earth' or 'land').

Beginning in the Cretaceous, when dinosaurs ruled the world, Pangaea split up into smaller pieces which slowly drifted apart. Alfred collected lots of evidence to support his idea:

✓ Layers of rock on different continents match up. This makes sense if they formed in the same place.

✓ Fossils of tropical, water-loving plants were found in places that are dry deserts today. This makes sense if the continents were once in different places.

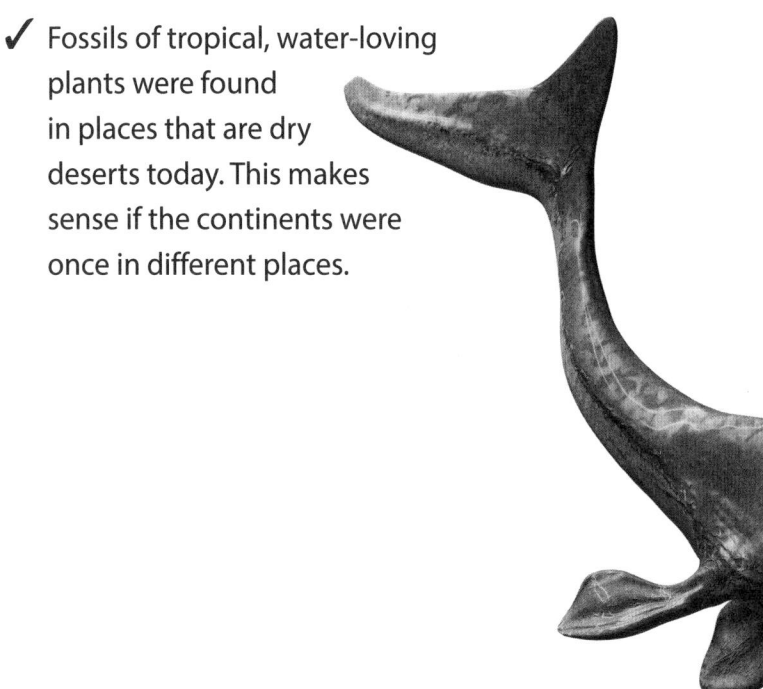

✓ The fossils of certain animals – such as mesosaurs – were found only in Southern Africa and Eastern South America, on opposite sides of the vast Atlantic Ocean. This medium-sized freshwater reptile would not have been able to swim across an ocean, so the fossil discoveries only make sense if these places were once joined.

However, one thing didn't make sense: Alfred couldn't explain HOW giant continents can possibly move around. It was another 30 years before scientists found the answer and proved Alfred right.

mesosaur

On the move

Don't be fooled by our planet's hard, rocky crust … deep below the surface, Earth has a semi-solid layer, known as the mantle!

The rocks of Earth's crust don't form a solid shell around the planet. They're broken up into 15 huge pieces called tectonic plates, which fit together like a giant jigsaw.

The plates float on top of the mantle. As the squishy rock of the mantle slowly moves about, the plates move too. They carry Earth's continents with them!

Fact
Plates move at around the same speed that fingernails grow – just a few centimetres every year.

The movement of the tectonic plates is usually too slow to notice. However, over millions of years, tiny changes add up to a big difference. It explains why Earth's continents are in different places today than they were 200 million years ago. It also explains why we might find fossils in unexpected places!

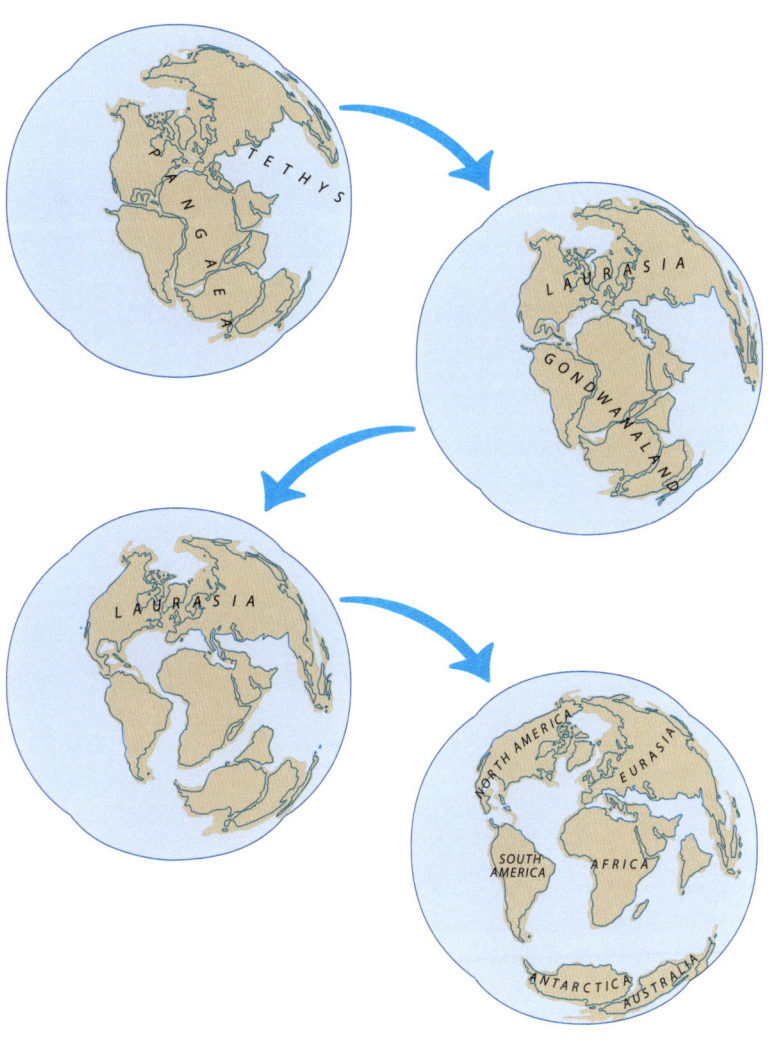

Case study

In 2024, Liam and Wade were digging in their school playground in West Virginia, USA, when they dug up a rock with a strange pattern.

Their teacher identified it as a fossil of an extinct tree, that once grew in tropical forests. Today, West Virginia is much cooler, with summer and winter temperatures similar to those in the UK.

This fossilised tree root is similar to the one Liam and Wade found.

Case study

In 1821, bones of hyenas, elephants, hippos and tigers were found in a limestone cave in Yorkshire, England. This is thousands of kilometres north of where these animals live today.

William Buckland – the first scientist to describe and name a dinosaur – was also one of the first people to realise that Britain must have once had a tropical climate, with completely different types of wildlife. This helped change the way people thought about the age of Earth and how habitats and life change over time.

How Yorkshire might have looked in the past.

Dinosaur habitats

Not all dinosaurs lived at the same time, and they didn't all live in the same part of the world. As the supercontinent Pangaea broke up and the continents drifted to new locations, dinosaurs had to adapt to many different and new habitats.

When the rock under your school formed, the land could have been in a completely different part of the world. The climate could have been much hotter or cooler. It could have been a jungle or a desert, or even an ocean!

This would have affected what kinds of creatures lived there, and what kinds of fossils might be found today.

Small meat-eating dinosaurs such as Coelophysis lived in the warm, dry Triassic. Its arms and claws helped it grab prey, while its super-sharp serrated teeth delivered a deadly bite.

Large, plant-eating dinosaurs such as Stegosaurus became common in the forests of the Jurassic, where there were lots of ferns and horsetails to eat. They even swallowed stones to help them grind up these tough plants!

Huge fish-eating dinosaurs like Spinosaurus thrived in the steamy swamps of the Cretaceous. Scientists think their huge 'sails' helped them keep cool.

Fast two-legged dinosaurs like Gallimimus sprinted across dry deserts in the Cretaceous. Their beaks helped them eat anything they came across, including plants and insects, while their long legs helped them avoid becoming lunch for other dinosaurs!

What if the rock under your school formed at the bottom of an ocean?

Dinosaurs were land animals, but sometimes they happened to die on the shores of shallow seas and became covered with sediments to form fossils. This means that dinosaur fossils are sometimes found even in sedimentary rocks that formed at the bottom of seas and oceans.

Case study

In 2012, pupils at a school in West Sussex, UK, discovered hundreds of fossils in rubble excavated by builders at their school. The fossils were embedded in sandstone, siltstone and limestone rocks from the Cretaceous period. They included snails, shells, crocodile teeth, scales and bones from ancient fish … and a dinosaur tooth!

a prehistoric crocodile

Finding dinosaur fossils

Palaeontologists look at geological maps to find out where there might be a chance of finding a dinosaur. Then they go to those places and start digging!

But even if you discover your school IS built on sedimentary rock from the Triassic, Jurassic and Cretaceous, you CAN'T just start digging through the playground or dining hall floor!

Luckily you don't have to, because fossils come up to the surface in lots of different ways …

CHAPTER 5
Finding fossils without digging

Scientists have dug up large numbers of dinosaur fossils in very dry areas of North America, China and South America. In these deserts and badlands, few plants grow and there's not much soil over the rocks.

Digging into words
'Badlands' are dry, rocky landscapes, with very hot summers and very cold winters. The name comes from the American Indian Lakota phrase *mako sica*, meaning 'bad lands' to travel through.

Other fossils – like the ones found under San Pedro High School – have been uncovered by accident, by people digging into sedimentary rock for other reasons.

In 2016, builders working next to a school in Jiangxi Province, China, blasted through rock using the explosive TNT. They uncovered fossils of arm, tail and leg bones, which turned out to belong to a brand-new type of dinosaur! Unfortunately, blasting through the rock damaged the fossils.

The newly discovered dinosaur is a birdlike raptor that lived between 72 and 66 million years ago.

However, fossils can also be found much nearer the surface, and without diggers or dynamite!

Case study

In 2021, six-year-old Siddak Singh Jhamat was sifting through soil in his garden in Walsall, UK, when he found a horn-shaped rock. It turned out to be the fossil of a 488-million-year-old coral! The fossil formed back when all of the world's land was part of the supercontinent Pangaea, and the rock that now lies under Siddak's garden was under an ocean!

horn coral fossils, similar to the one Siddak found

So how did the fossil get out of the rock and into the soil?

Rocks on the move

As Earth's giant tectonic plates drift about, they don't just shift continents from place to place. They can also push rocks deep underground or lift them up towards the surface.

These changes happen at the places where tectonic plates meet.

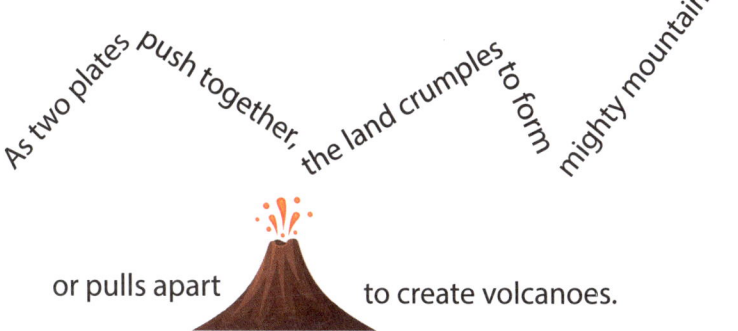

As two plates push together, the land crumples to form mighty mountains...

or pulls apart to create volcanoes.

Sometimes, one plate slides under another, lifting huge areas of the other plate upwards.

When these things happen, deeply-buried sedimentary rocks can be brought nearer the surface. When land crumples, layers that were once flat and horizontal might become vertical!

Worn away by water

The second thing that can bring fossils to the surface is **erosion**. Over long stretches of time, water and wind wear away the top layers of Earth's crust. This reveals the deeper layers underneath. It can reveal fossils that have been hidden for millions or billions of years.

Erosion happens fastest in areas where water is moving quickly.

Rushing rivers can carve a path through even the hardest rocks. Fossils can often be found in the steep walls of valleys and canyons.

Along coasts, crashing waves wear away the rocky land, creating cliffs that gradually crumble into the sea.

Valleys and coasts are popular places to look for fossils. Digging into cliffs or canyon walls is dangerous and not allowed. But in these places, it's possible to find fossils that have been washed out of the nearby rock.

Digging into words

The word 'erosion' comes from the Latin word *erodere*, meaning 'to gnaw away'. It describes how wind and water 'gnaw away' at rocks! The same Latin word inspired the name rodent, to describe a group of animals that like to nibble at things!

Case study

In 2003, 11-year-old Emily Cameron was on a school trip to the Isle of Wight, UK, when she came across a fossil footprint on the beach. Experts at the Isle's Dinosaur Museum confirmed it was the footprint of a huge Iguanodon, a dinosaur that lived in the area 125 million years ago.

a footprint similar to the one Emily found

Case study

In 2021, four-year-old Lily Wilder spotted the best dinosaur footprint fossil ever found in Wales, while walking along a beach with her family! She was searching for shells on the beach at Bendricks Bay when she uncovered the ten-centimetre footprint. It was made by a plant-eating dinosaur that lived in the area around 220 million years ago.

Case study

In 2020, 11-year-old Ruby Reynolds found part of the jawbone of a giant ichthyosaur on a beach in Somerset, England. One of the pieces of jaw was more than two metres long, and when scientists studied the bones, they realised Ruby had discovered a new species!

an ichthyosaur jawbone

Case study

In 2020, 12-year-old Nathan Hrushkin spotted fossil dinosaur bones in the walls of Horseshoe Canyon, Canada. He and his dad alerted experts, who discovered another 50 bones and worked out that they came from a hadrosaur (duck-billed dinosaur) that lived in the area 69 million years ago.

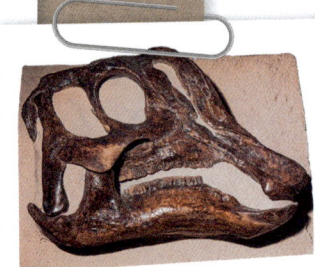

a hadrosaur skull

Case study

In 2024, ten-year-old Elana found a giant megalodon tooth on Bawdsey Beach in Suffolk, UK, while she was sifting through sand and mud. The ten-centimetre fossil most likely came from a teenage megalodon that was already ten to 12 metres long when it lost its tooth!

a megalodon tooth next to a shark tooth

Warning

Fossil hunters have to be very careful on beaches and near cliffs. Deep water and falling rocks can be very dangerous. Mary Anning was a famous fossil hunter in the 1800s. She collected fossils from the cliffs in Dorset, England. One day, she was nearly crushed by rocks falling from a cliff, and her pet dog Tray sadly died.

Mary Anning and Tray

From rocks to soil

Soil is the skin that covers Earth's rocky crust. Around half of soil is made up of tiny pieces of rocks and minerals. These are mixed with pockets of air, water, decaying plants and animals, and living creatures, such as worms!

As rocks are worn away by water and wind, they get broken into smaller pieces. These pieces might get washed into rivers and seas, or they might become part of the soil.

As you dig deeper in the soil, you might find larger chunks of rock. Most of these come from the **bedrock** that lies beneath the soil layer. As this rock gets broken down by water and plant roots, it becomes part of the soil. If there are fossils in the bedrock, these can make their way into the soil too!

Remember to wash your hands after touching soil. It's full of living creatures, including microbes. Just a teaspoon of soil can contain a billion bacteria!

What should I do if I find a fossil?

Don't just start hammering at it! Palaeontologists use tools to carefully remove the rock from around the fossil. And don't throw the rock away either. It can tell you what type of environment the fossil lived in. A sandstone rock may have formed near a beach or at the bottom of a river. A mudstone rock may have formed from the mud at the edge of a lake.

Case study

In 2025, a boy called Duke found the fossil of a marine mollusc while digging in his primary school's forest school area, in Shropshire, UK. The fossil was still embedded in a chunk of limestone rock. Experts looked at the rock and explained that it must have been carried to Shropshire by glaciers (giant rivers of slow-moving ice) during the last Ice Age!

Interview with Mary Anning

When did you start collecting fossils?

I was born in Dorset, one of the best places in the world to find fossils! My dad taught me how to find them on the beach, near crumbling cliffs. He was a carpenter and the cabinets he made were perfect for displaying fossils. Sadly, he died of tuberculosis when I was 11, and after that, selling fossils was one of the only ways my family could make money.

What is your most famous discovery?

When I was 12, my brother spotted an enormous skull sticking out of a cliff. I was determined to dig it out of the rock and ended up finding the entire skeleton! The skull alone was two metres long and looked a bit like the head of a crocodile.

What happened next?
We sold it to scientists in London for £23 (about £2,370 in today's money). It took them years to work out that it was the fossil of a sea creature that lived 200 million years ago. It was named Ichthyosaurus.

How did you become a fossil expert yourself?
I decided to teach myself everything I could about rocks and animals. This helped me understand the fossils I was finding and work out what these creatures looked like when they were alive. I became such an expert on coprolites (fossilised animal poo) that leading scientists travelled to Dorset to learn from me!

What are your top tips for fossil hunters?
Visit beaches as the tide is going down and look for fossils on the sand. But don't ever go near the cliffs themselves. I was so upset when part of a cliff fell upon my dog Tray and killed him.

CHAPTER 6
Finding fossils INSIDE your school!

If you can't find fossils under your school, try looking inside the building itself!

Sedimentary rocks are used to make all kinds of useful things, including buildings themselves. If fossils happen to be in the rocks, they can end up indoors too!

Case study

In 2025, a school in Queensland, Australia, turned out to have some of Australia's best dinosaur fossils sitting in the corner! The fossils were footprints on a large slab of rock that was given to the school as a gift. It had decorated the school office for more than 20 years. People had noticed that the boulder was covered in footprints, but it was only when a dinosaur expert began working nearby that they began to investigate.

The small, three-toed footprints turned out to be made by more than 47 small, plant-eating dinosaurs, that ran across a shallow, muddy stream 200 million years ago.

If there are no huge, footprint-covered boulders inside your school, where else might you find sedimentary rocks and fossils?

Fossils in the art cupboard

Every time you pick up a piece of chalk, you are holding thousands of fossils in your hand! Chalk is a sedimentary rock that formed in the Cretaceous, when the dinosaurs were still alive. It is mostly made from the skeletons of tiny sea creatures, which sunk to the bottom of the ocean between 100 and 60 million years ago. Over time, thick layers of this sludge were squeezed and heated, becoming sedimentary rock.

If you look at super close-up pictures of chalk taken with a **scanning electron microscope**, it's possible to see these tiny 'microfossils'. A piece of chalk just one millimetre across can contain 30,000 microfossils!

Fossils of much bigger creatures are sometimes found in chalky rocks, too. They include ammonites, sea urchins and sponges. Fossils of fish, pterosaurs, ichthyosaurs, plesiosaurs and turtles have been found too. So have the fossils of dinosaurs, which sometimes got washed out to sea after they died.

ammonite fossil

living nautilus

Ammonites are the fossilised shells of creatures related to today's octopuses and nautiluses.

Digging into words

'Ammonites' are named after the ancient Egyptian god Amun (or Ammon), who had curled horns on his head. They are also known as 'snakestones' because people in medieval Europe thought they were serpents that had been turned to stone!

Fossils in the sand tray

Sedimentary rocks like sandstone are formed from sand. When these rocks get eroded, they can become sand again. Sand often contains tiny fossils that are less than two millimetres across! From a distance, they look like any other grain of sand. Under a powerful microscope, you can see they are many different shapes and sizes.

tiny microfossils in sand

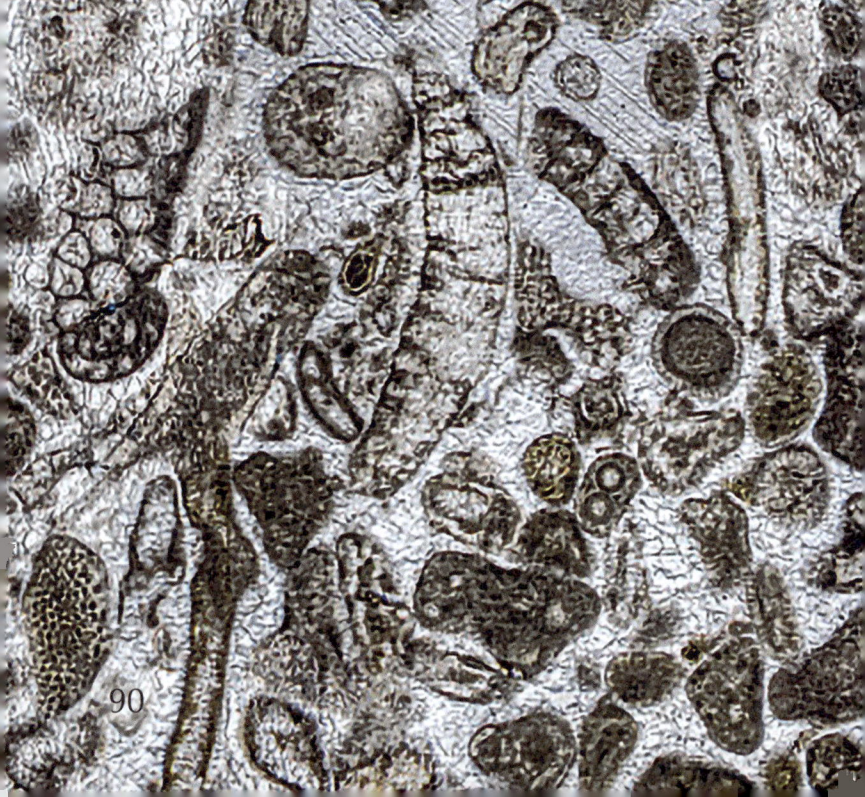

Fossils in the wildlife garden

Soil is full of tiny fossils! As well as microfossils less than two millimetres in size, you can find medium-sized mesofossils which measure from two millimetres to one centimetre (about pea-sized).

Digging into words
The prefix 'meso-' comes from the Greek word *mesos*, meaning 'middle'.

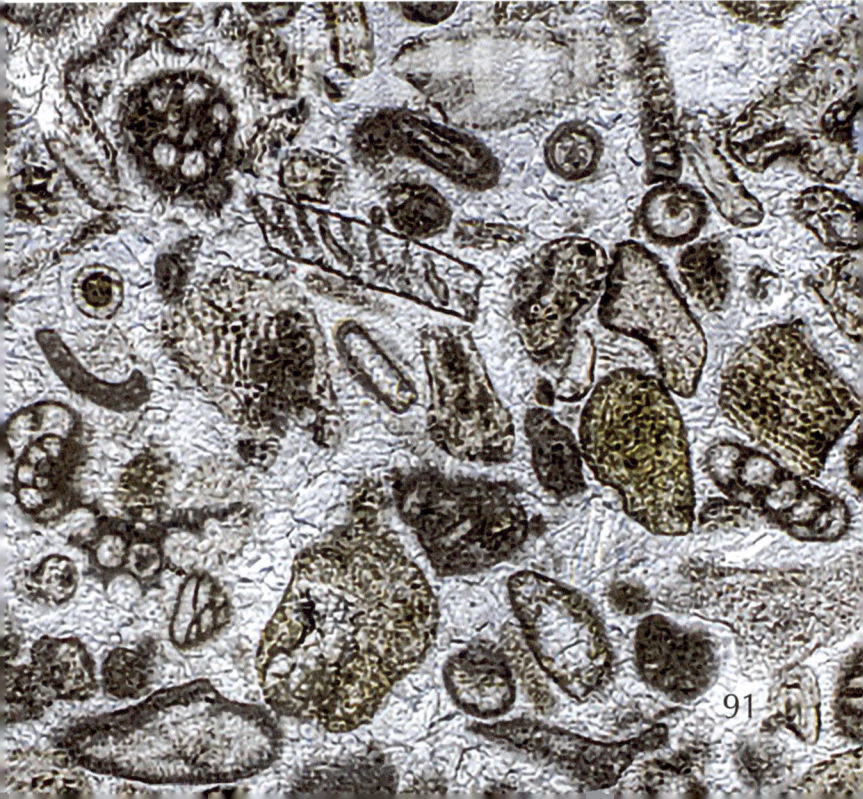

How to collect tiny fossils

1. Put a handful of soil into a jar of water. Leave it until all the sediments have settled.

2. Pour off as much water as possible. Remove any large bits of plants. Tip the remaining sediments into a sieve and rinse them with clean water.

3. Spread the sediments out on a dark-coloured tray. When they are dry, look at them under a magnifying glass.

4. If you spot a fossil, use a small, damp paintbrush to pick it up and put it onto a different tray.

1. bits of dead plants
2. water
3. tiny grains and clay
4. sand and silt
5. large lumps settle to the bottom

Sometimes, scientists find hundreds of tiny fossils in a single handful of soil!

Sand microfossils roughly 0.05 to 2 mm in size.

They might include:

- parts of a larger fossil that's been worn down by weathering
- complete fossils of tiny creatures
- tiny teeth of mammals, dinosaurs, lizards and snakes
- minute pollen fossils.

Tiny fossils help scientists work out which plants and animals were living in an area millions of years ago. They can help palaeontologists understand the habitats dinosaurs lived in.

Scientists at the University of Manchester used a SEM (scanning electron microscope) to spot a tiny fossil of a mite on a 50-million-year-old fossilised spider!

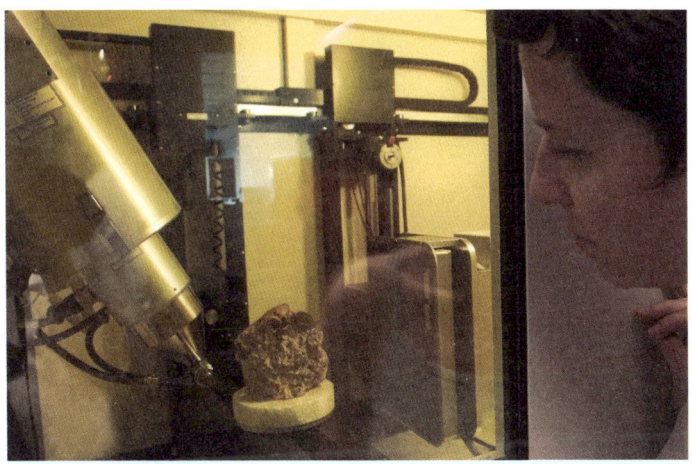

a SEM in action

Very tiny fossils have even helped the police solve crimes! If they find exactly the same tiny fossils in the soil of a crime scene and in the soil on someone's shoes, they can prove the person was at the crime scene.

Fossils in the walls and floor

Sedimentary rocks have been used in construction for thousands of years. The ancient Egyptian pyramids are made of giant blocks of sandstone and limestone.

Hundreds of thousands of fossils have been spotted in the stone. They include fossils of ancient sea-stars and sea urchins.

Sandstone and limestone are used to make modern buildings too. The British Library in London has fossils in its floors and walls.

Fossils can also be spotted in limestone pavements and shop floors. In Inverness, Scotland, a paving slab has been worn down by footsteps, revealing fossils of ancient fish!

Find out if any of the walls or floors in your school are made from limestone or sandstone. If so, you might spot fossils in them!

Fossils all around

Coal, oil and natural gas are known as 'fossil fuels'. This isn't just a name – they really are formed from fossils!

Millions of years ago, Earth was wetter and warmer than today. The land was covered in swampy forests. When the plants and trees died, they fell in the water and didn't start to **decompose** right away. Over time, they got buried by new layers of sediments. The water was squeezed out by the pressure from the layers above, and the dead plants slowly turned to **peat**, and then coal.

Oil and natural gas were formed when tiny plants and animals died and sank to the bottom of the sea. As new layers of sediments settled on top, the plant remains were squeezed with enormous pressure. They were also heated by rocks deep in Earth's crust. Slowly, they changed into oil and gas.

Burning fossil fuels unlocks the energy of the Sun captured by ancient plants. Fossil fuels might be used to heat your school, or to cook with in the kitchen.

drilling for oil

Lots of everyday items are made using fossil fuels, too.

laptop, crayons, pen, artificial grass, shoes, backpack, tyre

Just like other fossils, fossil fuels take millions of years to form. Once we have used them, it's impossible to replace them. One day, fossil fuels will run out.

Happy fossil hunting

Fossils are hidden all around us. They might be in the rock beneath your school. You might even spot them INSIDE your school!

By answering these questions, you can even discover if DINOSAUR FOSSILS might be lurking beneath your dining hall:

- What kind of rock is my school built on?
- How old is the rock?
- Where in the world is my school … and did dinosaurs live here in the past?

Next time you're charging around the playground, you might be following in the footsteps of prehistoric creatures!

Bonus

Surprising sedimentary rocks

These everyday things are made using sedimentary rocks, which mean they could also contain traces of fossils!

Tofu is made with the help of a very soft rock called gypsum. It helps the main ingredient of tofu clump together.

tofu

Bread and breakfast cereals are often **fortified** using limestone, which is rich in the mineral calcium.

breakfast cereal

bread

Powdered limestone or chalk is added to toothpaste to help scrub teeth clean.

Limestone powder is also added to some types of chewing gum.

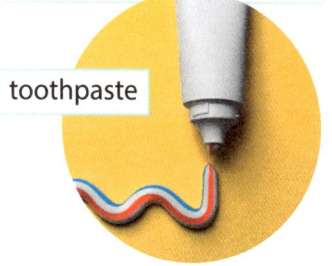
toothpaste

chewing gum

Chalk is used to help make paper bright white.

toilet paper

Make-up products such as bronzing powder are often made using a soft sedimentary rock that's made up of the fossils of tiny sea creatures called diatoms!

make-up

Glossary

bedrock the layer of solid rock underneath the soil layer

Cretaceous the last period of the Mesozoic era, when dinosaurs were alive (lasting from around 145 to 66 million years ago)

decompose decay or rot

earth scientist someone who studies Earth and its water and air

erosion the process by which rock is broken down and worn away by water and wind

extinct when there are no living members of a species left

fortified when vitamins and minerals are added to flour before it is used to make bread or cereals, to help keep people healthy

Jurassic the middle period of the Mesozoic era, when dinosaurs were alive (lasting from around 200 to 145 million years ago)

marine lives in the sea or to do with the sea

microbes tiny living things that can only be seen with the help of a microscope

minerals naturally occurring substances that are not alive

molten in liquid form, due to being heated

palaeontologist a scientist who studies fossil plants or animals

peat a special type of soil that forms when plants die in swamps, bogs or fens and don't completely decompose

prehistoric from before people began keeping written records of things

scanning electron microscope a very powerful microscope that uses beams of tiny particles (called electrons) instead of light, to take very close up pictures of tiny things

Triassic the first period of the Mesozoic era, when dinosaurs were alive (lasting from around 252 to 201 million years ago)

vertebrae the small bones that form the backbone or spine of an animal

About the author

Have you always been interested in dinosaurs?

When I was 13 years old, a film called *Jurassic Park* came out. It was the first film ever to use CGI and animatronics to create realistic dinosaurs. I was awestruck, and ever since then I (and millions of other people!) have wanted to find out more about dinosaurs.

Isabel Thomas

How did you hear about the school in San Pedro where they found the fossils?

I like to read the latest science and nature news, and this story caught my eye last year. The headline was '"Entire ecosystem" of fossils 8.7 million years old found under Los Angeles high school'. It made me want to find out more!

Have you ever found a fossil?

I have found lots! The most recent were beautiful iron pyrite ammonite fossils, which I found lying on Charmouth Beach in Dorset – one of the beaches Mary Anning used to fossil hunt on! I have also found belemnites (ancient squid fossils) and Gryphaea (ancient oyster fossils).

Do you have a favourite dinosaur?

I really like Therizinosaurus, because its claws were almost a metre long! Scientists think that Therizinosaurus used them to strim leaves from high-up branches.

How do you write books like this?
Most of my books start with a question that I really want to know the answer to! Next, I work out which smaller questions I will need to answer in order to help answer my BIG question. This guides my research. As I look for answers to these small questions, I keep careful notes about the most impressive, amazing or strange things I find out. Then I make sure all of those 'best bits' go into the book.

Where do you like to write?
I have a little study at home. It's packed with books, and I share it with two tortoises, so there is not much space to do anything EXCEPT write!

Do you have a favourite fact in this book?
I love the fact that the Great Pyramids in Egypt have fossils hidden in their giant stones! I would love to know what the ancient Egyptians thought of fossils.

What do you think is the most interesting fossil find in this book? Why?
I love the story of Elana, who found the giant megalodon tooth on a Suffolk beach. The beach is not far from where I live, so I would like to take my own children on a fossil-hunting trip. Every science writer would LOVE to find a megalodon tooth.

What do you hope readers get from this book?
I hope the book turns you into a dinosaur detective! Your local area is full of clues about both history and prehistory, and something as simple as a stone you find in the playground could be the beginning of an exciting discovery.

Book chat

What do you like about the title of this book?

If you had to think up a new title for the book, what would you choose?

Have you ever found a fossil?

Would you like to go fossil hunting? Why or why not?

Do you have a favourite dinosaur?

Had you heard about any of these discoveries before reading the book?

What did you know about dinosaurs before reading this book?

Who would you recommend this book to and why?

What have you learned from reading this book?

What do you think is the most interesting fossil find in this book? Why?

Would you like to read more books on fossils and dinosaurs?

What question would you ask the author if you could?

What do you enjoy about reading non-fiction?

Do you have a favourite fact from the book?

Did anything in this book surprise you? What was it?

Summarise this book in one sentence!

Book challenge:

Find a rock and use the rock key to identify which family it belongs to.

Published by Collins
An imprint of HarperCollins*Publishers*

The News Building
1 London Bridge Street
London
SE1 9GF
UK

Macken House
39/40 Mayor Street Upper
Dublin 1
D01 C9W8
Ireland

© HarperCollins*Publishers* Limited 2025

10 9 8 7 6 5 4 3 2 1

ISBN 978-0-00-879623-5

All rights reserved. No part of this publication may be reproduced, stored in a retrieval system, or transmitted in any form by any means, electronic, mechanical, photocopying, recording or otherwise, without the prior written permission of the Publisher or a licence permitting restricted copying in the United Kingdom issued by the Copyright Licensing Agency Ltd, 5th Floor, Shackleton House, 4 Battle Bridge Lane, London SE1 2HX.

Without limiting the exclusive rights of any author, contributor or the publisher of this publication, any unauthorised use of this publication to train generative artificial intelligence (AI) technologies is expressly prohibited. HarperCollins also exercise their rights under Article 4(3) of the Digital Single Market Directive 2019/790 and expressly reserve this publication from the text and data mining exception.

British Library Cataloguing-in-Publication Data
A catalogue record for this publication is available from the British Library.

Download the teaching notes and word cards to accompany this book at:
http://littlewandle.org.uk/signupfluency/

Get the latest Collins Big Cat news at
collins.co.uk/collinsbigcat

Author: Isabel Thomas
Comic strip illustrator: James Cottell
Publisher: Laura White
Product managers: Caroline Green and Holly Woolnough
Series editor: Charlotte Raby
Development editor: Catherine Baker
Commissioning editor: Suzannah Ditchburn
Project manager: Emily Hooton
Copyeditor: Sally Byford
Proofreader: Catherine Dakin
Cover designer: Sarah Finan
Typesetter: 2Hoots Publishing Services Ltd
Production controller: Sophie Waeland

Printed in the UK.

This book contains FSC™ certified paper and other controlled sources to ensure responsible forest management.

For more information visit: www.harpercollins.co.uk/green

Made with responsibly sourced paper and vegetable ink

Scan to see how we are reducing our environmental impact.

Acknowledgements
The publishers gratefully acknowledge the permission granted to reproduce the copyright material in this book. Every effort has been made to trace copyright holders and to obtain their permission for the use of copyright material. The publishers will gladly receive an information enabling them to rectify any error or omission at the first opportunity.

Front cover Tanes Ngamsom/Shutterstock, pp6–7 Christian Darkin, Science Photo Library, p9 Envicom Corporation/Dr Wayne Bischoff p10bl Millard H. Sharp/Science Photo Library, p11tl kampee patisena/Getty Images, p11c Detlev Van Ravenswaay/Science Photo Library, p15 Historic Images/Alamy, p18 Emma Nicholls/Oxford University Museum of Natural History, p19 Science Photo Library/Alamy, p21 Universal Pictures/Handout/Getty Images, p35 Dorling Kindersley ltd/Alamy, p36t Keith Jardine/Alamy, p37 Chris Craggs/Alamy, p44 Sorin Colac/Alamy, p45 Didier Dutheil/Getty Images, p46 INTERFOTO/Alamy, p48c B Christopher/Alamy, p48bl MasPix/Alamy, p48br Christian Jegou/Science Photo Library, p49tl Masato Hattori/Science Photo Library, p49tr & bl Stocktrek Images, Inc./Alamy, p49bl Stocktrek Images, Inc./Alamy, p49bc Christian Jegou Science Photo Library, p49br Richard Bizley/Science Photo Library, p50 & 51 Deagostini/UIG/Science Photo Library, p52 & 53 Richard Bizley/Science Photo Library, p56tl Antonio Gravante/Alamy, p57c & cr & br Antonio Gravante/Alamy, p59tl mark Turner/Alamy, p59tr Ray Troll, p61 Alfred Wegener, p67 B Christopher/Alamy, p68 Universal Images Group North America LLC/DeAgostini/Alamy, p71 Michael Rosskothen/Alamy, p73 Junchang Lü, Rongjun Chen, Stephen L. Brusatte, Yangxiao Zhu & Caizhi Shen, p76 Image Source Limited/Alamy, p78 Jonathan Player/Alamy, p79 Dean Lomax/The University of Manchester, p80t Millard H. Sharp/Science Photo Library, p81 Pictorial Press Ltd/Alamy, p83 Elizabeth Nunn/Alamy, p84t The History Collection/Alamy, p84b Ed Gorochowski/Alamy, p85 Nature Picture Library/Alamy, p87 Universal Images Group North America LLC/DeAgostini/Alamy, p88b Science Photo Library/Alamy, p89l Panther Media Global/Alamy, pp90–91 Alex Hyde/Nature Picture Library/Alamy, p93 DK Images/Science Photo Library, p94 Steve Gschmeissner/Science Photo Library, p95 Pascal Goetgheluck/Science Photo Library, p97 Simona Abbondio/Alamy, p101 Picture Partners/Alamy, back cover Daniel K. Driskill/Shutterstock. All other photos – Shutterstock.